★ ★

KANSAS

by William David Thomas

GARETH**STEVENS**
GS
PUBLISHING
A Member of the WRC Media Family of Companies

Please visit our web site at: www.garethstevens.com
For a free color catalog describing Gareth Stevens Publishing's
list of high-quality books and multimedia programs, call
1-800-542-2595 (USA) or 1-800-387-3178 (Canada).
Gareth Stevens Publishing's fax: (414) 332-3567.

Library of Congress Cataloging-in-Publication Data

Thomas, William, 1947–
    Kansas / William David Thomas.
        p. cm. — (Portraits of the states)
    Includes bibliographical references and index.
    ISBN 0-8368-4665-6 (lib. bdg.)
    ISBN 0-8368-4684-2 (softcover)
    1. Kansas—Juvenile literature. I. Title. II. Series.
    F681.3.T475   2006
    978.1—dc22   2005054340

This edition first published in 2006 by
Gareth Stevens Publishing
A Member of the WRC Media Family of Companies
330 West Olive Street, Suite 100
Milwaukee, WI 53212 USA

This edition copyright © 2006 by Gareth Stevens, Inc.

Editorial direction: Mark J. Sachner
Project manager: Jonatha A. Brown
Editor: Catherine Gardner
Art direction and design: Tammy West
Picture research: Diane Laska-Swanke
Indexer: Walter Kronenberg
Production: Jessica Morris and Robert Kraus

Picture credits: Cover, pp. 4, 20, 24, 26, 27 © John Elk III; p. 5 © PhotoDisc; pp. 6,
12 © MPI/Getty Images; p. 8 © Hulton Archive/Getty Images; p. 10 © Corel; pp. 15,
18, 25 © Gibson Stock Photography; p. 16 © Carl Iwasaki/Time & Life Pictures/Getty
Images; p. 22 © Larry W. Smith/Getty Images; p. 29 © Andy Lyons/Getty Images

Printed in the United States of America

1 2 3 4 5 6 7 8 9 10 09 08 07 06

CONTENTS

Words that are defined in the Glossary appear
in **bold** the first time they are used in the text.

On the Cover: Kansas has a fitting nickname. It is called
"the Sunflower State."

Introduction

The official state song of Kansas, "Home on the Range," begins like this:

> "Oh give me a home
> Where the buffalo roam,
> Where the deer and the antelope play."

If you go to Kansas today, you will not see many buffalo. You will see big fields of wheat. You will see ranches, cowboys, and cattle. You also will see high rocks with strange shapes and flat land covered with tall grass. Kansas has large cities with tall buildings and factories where airplanes are built. It has a famous barbeque contest, too. The state has some fun museums and zoos (where the buffalo roam now). So come for a visit! Kansas is a great state.

No, it is not a giant mushroom. These big rocks are in Ellsworth County, Kansas.

The state flag of Kansas.

KANSAS FACTS

- Became the 34th U.S. State: January 29, 1861
- Population (2004): 2,735,502
- Capital: Topeka
- Biggest Cities: Wichita, Overland Park, Kansas City, Topeka
- Size: 81,815 square miles (211,901 square kilometers)
- Nickname: The Sunflower State
- State Flower: Sunflower
- State Tree: Cottonwood
- State Animal: American buffalo (bison)
- State Bird: Western meadowlark

History

Native American hunters were the first people in the area of Kansas. They came thousands of years ago. These early people followed herds of buffalo across the flat grasslands.

In 1541, a Spanish explorer named Francisco Vásquez de Coronado visited Kansas. He was looking for gold. Some of his horses were left behind. Native Americans caught them and soon became expert riders. Horses made it easier to hunt buffalo.

Many Indian groups lived in Kansas. Some of them were the Osage, Pawnee, and Wichita. Starting in about 1750, they were joined by the Kaw and Omaha tribes. White people forced the Natives off their

Francisco Vásquez de Coronado had heard stories about even cities made of gold. He looked for these cities in Kansas.

lands in the east. Native people had to move west.

Explorers and Settlers

For many years, France claimed the middle part of North America. In 1803, the United States bought this land. It was called the Louisiana Purchase, and Kansas was part of it.

White Americans reached Kansas in 1804. They were led by Meriwether Lewis and William Clark. Other explorers followed them. Soon, settlers moved to the area. From 1840 to 1860, three hundred thousand **pioneers** traveled across Kansas. Some of them stayed there. They built houses and started farms.

Slavery and Statehood

In the 1800s, the United States was divided over slavery. It was against the law in most Northern states. The Southern states wanted to keep slavery.

In 1854, Kansas was not a state. It was a **territory** of the United States. Soon, it would become a state. Leaders of the slave states wanted Kansas to be a slave state, too. Others wanted it to be a free state. Those who were against slavery were called "Free Soilers."

In 1856, men who wanted slavery attacked some Free Soilers in the town of

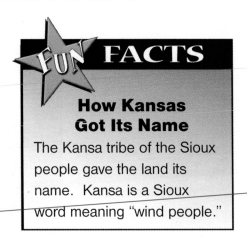

FACTS

How Kansas Got Its Name

The Kansa tribe of the Sioux people gave the land its name. Kansa is a Sioux word meaning "wind people."

Lawrence. They burned lots of homes. Even more fighting followed. Many people were killed. The fighting became so bad that people started to call this land "Bleeding Kansas." In 1859, the Free Soilers won. Slavery was outlawed. Kansas became a state in 1861.

The next year, Congress passed the Homestead Act. This law gave free land to settlers. They had to build a home and live on the land for five years. Then, the land was theirs. Many new settlers moved to Kansas because of this law.

IN KANSAS'S HISTORY

The Santa Fe Trail

In 1822, William Becknell opened a trail through Kansas. It was the first trail to the West that was wide and flat enough for wagons. This made it easier for settlers to travel. The trail began in Missouri and went across Kansas. Then it turned south toward New Mexico. Travelers called it the Santa Fe Trail. The famous Oregon Trail also passed through Kansas.

Native Americans were not allowed to claim any Homestead Act land. Many of them were forced out of the state. They went south

These soldiers fought for the South in the Civil War. Few battles took place in Kansas.

to an area known as Indian Territory. Today, that land is the state of Oklahoma.

Railroads and Cowboys

Railroads came to Kansas in 1868. The state's flat land was perfect for railroad tracks. Soon, the tracks crossed the state. The railroads made it easy to move goods from the West

African American Pioneers

The Civil War was fought from 1861 to 1865. When the war ended, all of the slaves in the nation were free. They could live where they wanted. Many freed slaves came to Kansas. One group started a town called Nicodemus. It was the first town west of the Mississippi River founded by African Americans. Today, it is a National Historic Site.

to the big markets in the eastern United States.

Texas did not yet have railroads. Cowboys began driving beef cattle from Texas to Kansas. In towns like Dodge City, Abilene, and Wichita, the cattle were loaded onto trains.

The cattle were then shipped to markets in the East. Between the years 1867 and 1886, more than eight million cattle were driven from Texas to Kansas.

Cattle towns could be dangerous places. Cowboys did lots of drinking, fighting, and shooting. Kansas was part of "the Wild West."

The Breadbasket

In 1874, settlers brought a new kind of wheat to the state. It was called Turkey Red. The weather and flat land in Kansas were good for growing this kind of wheat. Grasslands quickly became wheat fields. Mills were built. The mills ground wheat into flour for bread. Kansas became known as "the Breadbasket of the United States."

Oil was found in Kansas in 1892. Then, drilling for oil and natural gas became a big business. Cars were made in Kansas factories by the early 1900s. In the 1920s, Kansas workers built some of the world's first manufactured airplanes.

Hard Times

In the 1930s, prices for crops and goods fell. Banks closed. Millions of people lost their jobs. These years were known as the **Great Depression**. A drought came, too. This was a long time with little or no rain.

IN KANSAS'S HISTORY

The Last Buffalo

Buffalo were a problem for the railroads. They often blocked the tracks and stopped trains. Hunters were hired to kill the big animals. One hunter, William F. Cody, killed so many he was nicknamed "Buffalo Bill." Before settlers came, there were millions of buffalo in Kansas. By 1889, only eight hundred were left in all of the United States.

Buffalo were once an important source of food and hides for Native people in Kansas.

A Surprised Mayor

In 1887, the city of Argonia, Kansas, was choosing a new mayor. Susanna Salter got a big surprise when she voted. Her name was on the ballot! It had been placed there without her knowledge. She won the election. She was the first woman ever elected mayor of a U.S. city.

The soil became dry. It turned into dust and blew away. Kansas and the states nearby were called "The Dust Bowl." Crops died. Farmers lost their land and their homes.

World War II and Beyond

More rain fell after 1938, but jobs and money were still scarce. Then, in 1941, the United States entered

Famous People of Kansas

Dwight D. Eisenhower

Born: October 14, 1890, Dennison, Texas

Died: March 28, 1969, Washington, D.C.

Dwight "Ike" Eisenhower grew up in Abilene. He became a soldier. He served in the U.S. Army for more than thirty years. During World War II, he led the **Allied armies** in Europe. After the war, he ran for president of the United States. He was elected twice, in 1952 and 1956. People who voted for him wore buttons that said, "I like Ike." While he was president, Alaska and Hawaii became states.

In the 1930s, very dry land and strong winds made dust storms. This one covered the town of Elkhart in dust.

World War II. During the war, Kansas wheat and beef helped feed soldiers. Kansas factories built war planes. These businesses helped put people back to work. After the war, these factories kept growing. They made rockets and other parts for the U.S. space program.

Today, Kansas is famous for both its farms and its factories.

IN KANSAS'S HISTORY

Oliver Brown's Battle

In much of America in the 1950s, black children could not go to the same schools as white children. Oliver Brown, an African American man, lived in Topeka. He wanted his daughter to go to the white children's school. He took the school board to court. Brown's case reached the United States Supreme Court. In 1954, the court said that separate schools were wrong. Brown's case was one of the first steps toward equal rights for African Americans.

1541	Spanish explorers come to Kansas.
1804	The first American explorers visit Kansas.
1854	Kansas becomes a territory of the United States.
1856–1858	Groups for and against slavery fight each other.
1861	Kansas becomes the thirty-fourth U.S. state.
1862	The Homestead Act brings many new settlers.
1868	Railroads are built in Kansas.
1870–1886	Cowboys drive millions of cattle from Texas to the state's railroad towns.
1874	Wheat farming begins.
1892	Oil is found in Kansas.
1935–1938	Drought makes Kansas part of the "Dust Bowl."
1941–1945	World War II brings many jobs to Kansas.
1954	The U.S. Supreme Court case *Brown v. the Board of Education* helps African Americans get equal rights.
1996	Kansas Senator Bob Dole runs for president. He is defeated by Bill Clinton.

People

Kansas is a big state, but it has a small population. Fewer than three million people live there.

From Many Places

Until the mid-1800s, most of the people in Kansas were Native Americans. After the Civil War, lots of white settlers came. People moved to Kansas from the eastern United States. **Immigrants** came to the state from western and central Europe. The population of the state grew quickly.

Hispanics: In the 2000 Census, 7 percent of the people in Kansas called themselves Latino or Hispanic. Most of them or their relatives came from places where Spanish is spoken. They may come from different racial backgrounds.

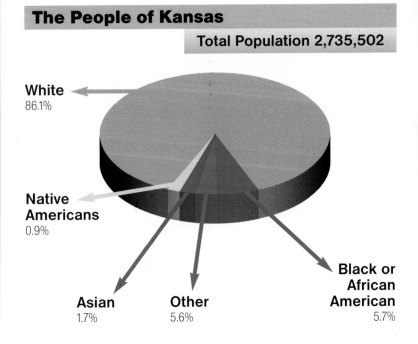

The People of Kansas

Total Population 2,735,502

White
86.1%

Native Americans
0.9%

Asian
1.7%

Other
5.6%

Black or African American
5.7%

Percentages are based on the 2000 Census.

Evening in downtown Witchita. It is the biggest city in Kansas.

In recent years, people from Mexico and Vietnam have come to live and work in the state of Kansas.

From Farm to City

In the early 1900s, most people in Kansas lived on farms or in small towns. That has changed. Fewer people earn their living by farming or ranching. Today, two-thirds of all the people in Kansas live in cities and large towns.

Famous People of Kansas

Robert Dole

Born: July 23, 1923, Russell, Kansas

Bob Dole was born and raised in Kansas. He was an officer in the U.S. Army during World War II. He was hurt while fighting in Italy. Dole got medals for bravery. He was a hero. After the war, he became a lawyer. In 1968, he was elected to the U.S. Senate. He worked in the Senate for many years and became a leader there. He ran for president in 1996, but lost to Bill Clinton.

In 1951, Oliver Brown took a school board to court so that his daughter Linda could go to school with white children.

Most of the large cities are in the eastern part of Kansas. The western part of the state is more **rural**. It has mostly small towns. Fewer people live there.

Religion and Education

More than nine out of ten people who live in Kansas are Christians. Some of the Christians are Roman Catholics. Most of them, however, are Protestants, like the first white settlers in the state. Other people are Jews, Buddhists, Hindus, and Muslims. A few people in the state practice Native American faiths.

The first schools in the state were built in the 1830s.

These schools were started by Christian missionaries. They wanted to educate Native American children. A few white children went to these schools, too.

In 1855, Kansas passed laws that made education free for all white children. The laws were changed in 1859. Then, all children received a free education.

Kansas has more than twenty-five colleges and universities. The largest is the University of Kansas, in Lawrence. Kansas State University, in Manhattan, is also very big. Both schools have more than twenty thousand students. Kansas also has many fine community colleges and job training schools.

Famous People of Kansas

Amelia Earhart

Born: July 24, 1897, Atchison, Kansas

Disappeared: July 2, 1937, over the Pacific Ocean

Amelia Earhart was a pioneer pilot. She was the first woman to fly alone across the Atlantic Ocean. She set a speed record doing it! Earhart was the first person to fly from Hawaii to California. In 1937, she and her copilot, Fred Noonan, tried to fly around the world. Near the end of the trip, while flying from New Guinea to Hawaii, her plane disappeared. Many people searched for Earhart, but she was never found.

The Land

Kansas lies in a part of the United States known as the Midwest. It is the thirteenth largest state. The state is a rectangle. It is about 400 miles (644 km) across and about 200 miles (322 km) from top to bottom.

A Dry Ocean

Kansas is one of the **Great Plains** states. This mostly flat land was once the bottom of an ocean. Now, however, water is sometimes scarce.

Farmers use water from Kansas's rivers to **irrigate** their crops. Some streams and rivers in western Kansas dry up during the long, hot summers. People have built dams across some

FUN FACTS

Sharks!

Scientists come to western Kansas to study **fossils**. These are the remains of sea animals that lived there millions of years ago. Most were small fish and other tiny creatures. But some were giant sharks that swam in the ocean there long ago.

These sail boats and motor boats are waiting to go! They are on Lake Clinton, near Lawrence.

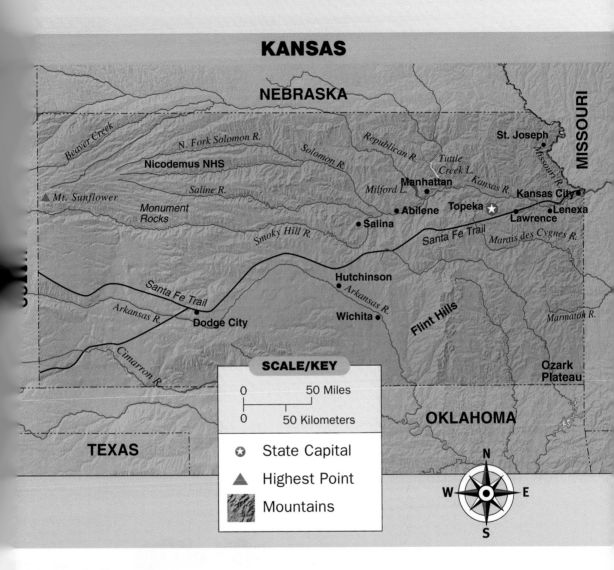

KANSAS

NEBRASKA

Beaver Creek

N. Fork Solomon R.

Nicodemus NHS

Solomon R.

Republican R.

St. Joseph

Missouri R.

Tuttle Creek L.

▲ Mt. Sunflower

Saline R.

Milford L.

Manhattan

Kansas R.

Kansas City

Monument Rocks

Abilene

Topeka ★

Lenexa

Lawrence

Salina

Smoky Hill R.

Santa Fe Trail

Marais des Cygnes R.

MISSOURI

Hutchinson

Santa Fe Trail

Arkansas R.

Wichita

Flint Hills

Marmaton R.

Arkansas R.

Dodge City

Cimarron R.

SCALE/KEY

| 0 | 50 Miles |
| 0 | 50 Kilometers |

✪ State Capital

▲ Highest Point

Mountains

Ozark Plateau

OKLAHOMA

TEXAS

N
W E
S

of the other rivers. Dams slow the flow of water. Lakes form behind the dams. Kansas has about 150 lakes.

A Great Variety of Land

Strangers to Kansas think the whole state is flat. This is not really true. The land in the east, near Missouri, is low. As it goes west toward the Rocky Mountains, the land rises. Many interesting features are found within the state's borders.

The Ozark **Plateau** is in the southeastern corner of

19

the state. This hilly area is covered with trees.

The Flint Hills are near Wichita. This is the largest area of unplowed **prairie** in the United States. Hundreds of native grasses grow there. Some of these plants are not found anywhere else in America.

The western part of Kansas is called post rock country. Early settlers found **limestone** there. Limestone is easy to cut. There were few trees, so the settlers made fence posts from the rock.

The state's highest point is Mt. Sunflower. It is near the western

Major Rivers
Missouri River
2,466 miles (3,968 km)
Arkansas River
1,450 miles (2,333 km)
Kansas (or Kaw) River
170 miles (273 km)

border with Colorado. The top of this mountain is 4,039 feet (1,231 meters) above sea level.

In southern Kansas are the Red Hills. Their name

The Kansas prairie is full of color. These grasses and wildflowers are near the Flint Hills.

comes from the color of the soil. It contains iron oxide. That is rust! These rusty-red hills are flat on top.

Climate

Summer in Kansas is usually very hot and dry. Winter can be very cold and windy, but there is not much snow. Western Kansas gets much less rain than the eastern part of the state.

Every summer, **tornadoes** come to Kansas. Special underground shelters have been built in many places. Children are taught to go to these shelters when they hear sirens warning that a dangerous storm is coming. The Great Plains have more tornadoes than any other place on Earth.

Birds, Animals, and Plants

Hundreds of different kinds of birds make their homes in

Right in the Middle

For many years, the exact center of the United States was near Lebanon, Kansas. This changed when Alaska and Hawaii became states.

Kansas. Some are small, like the meadowlark. It is the state bird. Other birds, such as the whooping crane and the bald eagle, are very large. Fields and hills are home to raccoons, squirrels, prairie dogs, and deer. The buffalo that once lived in the wild are gone. Now, they live on ranches and in zoos.

In spring and summer, pretty wildflowers pop up across the state. You can see pink and purple asters, blue columbines, and big yellow sunflowers.

Economy

Ninety percent of all the land in Kansas is used for farming. The state's farms grow crops and raise animals.

Twenty percent of all the wheat in the United States is grown in Kansas. It is first among all the states in making flour. Corn is another important crop.

At one time, cattle came to Kansas from Texas. Now, the state raises its own cattle. Packing plants turn the cattle into meat. Kansas beef is sent to restaurants and stores all over the country.

Airplanes and Energy

Wichita leads the world in making a kind of airplane called *personal aircraft*. They are small airplanes that can carry from

These airplanes are being built in a Wichita factory. The city was once called "the air capital of the world."

two to twenty people. Big factories in Kansas also turn out lots of cars.

Kansas helps the nation meet its energy needs. Oil from the state is made into gasoline. Natural gas from Kansas is used for heating and cooking.

Oil and gas are not the state's only natural resources. Hutchinson, Kansas, is one of the leading salt mining areas in the nation.

Services

The service industry is the biggest type of business in Kansas. More people work in service jobs than in any other kind of job. Service workers help other people. They run restaurants and stores. They work in hotels and movie theaters. Doctors and nurses have service jobs. Teachers and repair people have service jobs, too.

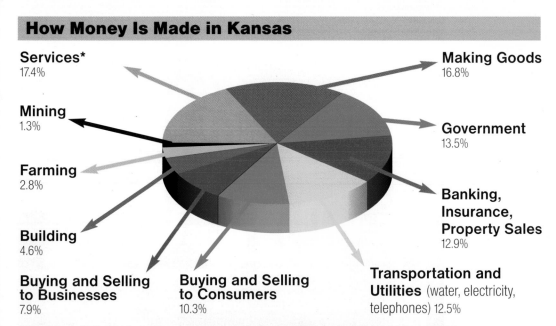

How Money Is Made in Kansas

Services*
17.4%

Making Goods
16.8%

Mining
1.3%

Government
13.5%

Farming
2.8%

Banking, Insurance, Property Sales
12.9%

Building
4.6%

Buying and Selling to Businesses
7.9%

Buying and Selling to Consumers
10.3%

Transportation and Utilities (water, electricity, telephones) 12.5%

* Services include jobs in hotels, restaurants, auto repair, medicine, teaching, and entertainment.

Government

Kansas's lawmakers and leaders work in Topeka, the capital city. The state government has three parts. They are the executive branch, the legislative branch, and the judicial branch.

Executive Branch

The governor leads the executive branch. The purpose of this branch is to carry out the laws of the state. The governor also picks a team of twelve people to work with him or her. This team is called the cabinet.

This is the State capitol building. It is in Topeka.

24

The governor of Kansas lives in this house. The land around it has nature trails and jogging paths. Anyone can use them.

Legislative Branch

The legislative branch makes the laws for the state. The House of Representatives and the Senate are the two parts of this branch.

Judicial Branch

Courts and judges make up the judicial branch. People charged with crimes go to court. Judges may decide if they are guilty. The State Supreme Court is the most important court in Kansas.

Local Government

Kansas has 105 counties. Each county chooses its leaders. They take care of roads, schools, water, and other services.

KANSAS'S STATE GOVERNMENT

Executive		Legislative		Judicial	
Office	**Length of Term**	**Body**	**Length of Term**	**Court**	**Length of Term**
Governor	4 years	Senate (40 members)	4 years	Supreme (7 justices)	6 years
Lieutenant Governor	4 years	House of Representatives (125 members)	2 years	Court of Appeals (12 judges)	4 years

Things to See and Do

If you visit Kansas, go outside! For swimming, boating, or camping, try one of Kansas's many lakes. If you come in the fall, watch the prairie grasses turn bright red. Or visit Monument Rocks, near Scott City. Some of the rocky arches and towers there are 60 feet (18 m) high.

From Animals to Oz

Kansas is for animal lovers. The zoo in Topeka is world famous. You can see a forest where bears and foxes live. A glass tunnel lets you get up close to the gorillas. At the Rolling Hills Refuge, near Salina, you can see camels, rhinos, and other animals.

Look at a modern jet fighter. Stand next to an old biplane. In this Topeka museum, you can see war planes from today and long ago.

Get your hands on some fun at Exploration Place in Wichita. At this special kid's museum, you can do things, not just look at them! Try piloting a plane in a **flight simulator**. Play with a huge electric train set.

If you like food cooked outdoors, visit the Great Lenexa Barbeque Battle in Lenexa. It is a contest to see who can grill the best chicken, steaks, and ribs.

FACTS

String and Wire

The world's largest ball of twine is in Cawker City. It has more than 1,300 miles (2,092 km) of string. A museum in LaCrosse has more than two thousand kinds of barbed wire.

You can relive the days of the Wild West at the Boot Hill museum. These buildings show what Dodge City looked like in the 1880s.

Famous People of Kansas

Walter Johnson

Born: November 6, 1887, Humboldt, Kansas

Died: December 10, 1946, Washington, D.C.

Walter Johnson was one of the greatest baseball players of all time. He was a pitcher. Because he was a big man and threw the ball very fast, he was called "The Big Train." Johnson pitched for the Washington Senators for twenty-one years. He led the league in strikeouts twelve times. He won 417 games. Only one pitcher ever won more. Johnson was one of the first five players voted into the Baseball Hall of Fame.

Every summer, people come from all over the country to take part. Others come just to watch and taste! This is just one of many festivals that take place in Kansas every year.

The movie *The Wizard of Oz* begins and ends in Kansas. A life-sized model of Dorothy's house, just as it was in the film, is in the town of Liberal. Right next door, you can walk through the Land of Oz.

Sports

Kansas sports fans are wild about their college teams. The University of Kansas is famous for men's basketball. The Jayhawks are one of the country's top teams nearly every year. College football is a popular sport in the state, too.

Kansas still celebrates its Wild West days. During the summer, many towns across the state have festivals and rodeos. Crowds cheer as riders rope calves and try to stay on bucking broncos.

Kansas plays Kentucky in this 2005 college game. The Jayhawks' Michael Lee drives to the basket! He shoots! He scores!

Famous People of Kansas

Gordon Parks

Born: November 30, 1912, Fort Scott, Kansas

Gordon Parks is a famous African American photographer. When he was young, he worked as a waiter on trains. He loved the magazine pictures that he saw as he worked. He taught himself to be a photographer. In 1941, he moved to Washington, D.C. There, he took photos that showed the hard lives of African Americans in the city. He took pictures for *Life* magazine for twenty-four years. Parks has also written books, poetry, and music. He has directed five movies, too.

★ ★

Allied armies — the armies of the United States, Canada, Britain, France, and the Soviet Union in World War II (1939–1945)

flight simulator — a machine that acts like an airplane, but doesn't leave the ground

fossils — the skeletons and other traces of animals and plants preserved in stone or clay

Great Depression — a time, in the 1930s, when many people lost jobs and businesses lost money

Great Plains — a big area of mostly flat land in the center of the United States

immigrants — people who leave one country to live in another country

irrigate — to bring water to fields through pipes, ditches, or canals

limestone — a type of rock that is formed mainly by once-living material, such as coral or shells

pioneers — some of the first to live in a new place

plateau — a large area of flat land that is higher than the land around it

prairie — a large area of mostly flat, grassy land

rural — belonging to the country or people who live in the countryside

territory — an area that belongs to a country

tornadoes — violent storms that have a dark cloud shaped like a funnel and strong, whirling wind

Books

Kansas. Seeds of a Nation (series). Patricia D. Netzley. (Thomson Gale)

Kansas. Welcome to the U.S.A. (series). Ann Heinrichs (Child's World)

Kansas Facts and Symbols. The States and Their Symbols (series). Kathleen W. Deady (Bridgestone)

Kansas Jeopardy. Questions and Answers About Our State. Carole Marsh (Gallopade International)

Pioneer Summer. Prairie Skies (series). Deborah Hopkinson. (Aladdin Library)

Prairie Day. My First Little House Books (series). Laura Ingalls Wilder (Sagebrush)

Web Sites

Enchanted Learning: Kansas
www.enchantedlearning.com/usa/states/kansas/

Kansas Secretary of State: Kansas Kids
www.kssos.org/resources/kansas_kids.html

Kansas State Historical Society
www.kshs.org/kids/

World Almanac for Kids: Kansas
www.worldalmanacforkids.com/explore/states/kansas.html

INDEX